Think With Your Heart

by Lexi Parker

Illustrations by Rose Bennington

For the families I've been lucky enough to work with.

Your effort, resilience, and love inspire me everyday.

More of your favorite characters from this series of books

Bob

Ralphie

Lana

Petey the Puffer Fish lived in Pacific Paradise.
He was a pleasant fish who loved going to school with his puffer pals.
But there was just one problem…

Petey would forget to think with his heart.
This meant he would forget to think about other puffers' feelings.
He would get excited and puff-up, accidently poking his pals.

He would gobble up the snack before the other puffers had a chance to eat theirs. And he would paddle to the front of the line, cutting in front of all of his pals.

One day, Ms. Pattie had an announcement,
"Today we will be having a party!" "Yay!" exclaimed the puffers.
Petey got excited and puffed up, accidently poking his pal Paco.

"Eek!" cried Paco. "I don't want to sit by Petey anymore.
He always pokes me." Paco swam away to the other side of the room.

Then Paige yelled out, "I don't like when Petey eats all of my snack!"
"Or when he cuts in front of me in line," Phil chimed in.

"I don't mean to!" Petey cried out and raced out of the classroom.
Ms. Pattie paddled out after him.
"Petey wait, I think I know what the problem is."

"What?" asked Petey. "You forget to think with your heart." explained Ms. Pattie. "Before you act, pause and think about how you would feel if a puffer did that to you."

"For instance, how would you feel if Paco poked you?" "Sad," said Petey. "I never thought about it like that." Ms. Pattie smiled, "Try to think with your heart today and see what happens." "I'll try my best," Petey said.

"Petey, go sit next to Paco," said Ms. Pattie.
"I have some more exciting news."

"Today's party is a plankton pizza party." "Yay!" the puffers exclaimed. Petey started to puff up with excitement, but then he paused to think with his heart. "How would I feel if Paco puffed up and poked me?"

Petey decided to paddle away from his pals to puff up. He swam back to sit next to Paco. Paco smiled, "Thanks for puffing up away from me Petey. You can sit next to me for the whole year if you want to." Petey smiled, he had always wanted to sit with a pal.

"Okay class. Time to line up and wash our fins."
Petey began to swim to the front of the line when he paused to think
with his heart. "How would I feel if someone cut in front of me?"

Petey spun around and swam to the back of the line behind Phil.
Phil turned around and gave Petey a big high-paddle,
"Good thinking Petey!"

The puffers had a blast at the party making their giant plankton pizza.

Petey was getting ready to gobble up the whole pizza, when he paused to think with his heart. 'How would I feel if someone ate my pizza?' Petey carefully made sure he only ate one slice.

"Wow Petey!" exclaimed Paige.
"You didn't gobble up my snack today. Good job!"
Petey smiled. "Thanks Paige."

Afterward, it was time for Ms. Pattie to announce the puffer of the month. "Today's puffer of the month goes to a special puffer who had a great day learning to think with his heart…"

"Petey!" Petey's eyes widened and his jaw dropped. "Yay!" his pals cheered. Petey paddled up to put his picture on the puffer of the month poster. 'Thinking with your heart is so much more fun' thought Petey.

Petey had learned how to think with his heart and had never felt happier.

THE END

www.ingramcontent.com/pod-product-compliance
Lightning Source LLC
Chambersburg PA
CBHW041242040426

42445CB00004B/122

9780985125639